A JOURNEY TOWARDS
HOPE

A JOURNEY TOWARDS
HOPE

LEE C. TIMMER

BALBOA.
PRESS

A DIVISION OF HAY HOUSE

Balboa Press books may be ordered through booksellers or by contacting:

Balboa Press
A Division of Hay House
1663 Liberty Drive
Bloomington, IN 47403
www.balboapress.com
1-(877) 407-4847

Because of the dynamic nature of the Internet, any web addresses or links contained in this book may have changed since publication and may no longer be valid. The views expressed in this work are solely those of the author and do not necessarily reflect the views of the publisher, and the publisher hereby disclaims any responsibility for them.

The author of this book does not dispense medical advice or prescribe the use of any technique as a form of treatment for physical, emotional, or medical problems without the advice of a physician, either directly or indirectly. The intent of the author is only to offer information of a general nature to help you in your quest for emotional and spiritual well-being. In the event you use any of the information in this book for yourself, which is your constitutional right, the author and the publisher assume no responsibility for your actions.

Any people depicted in stock imagery provided by Thinkstock are models, and such images are being used for illustrative purposes only.
Certain stock imagery © Thinkstock.

ISBN: 978-1-4525-3558-6 (e)
ISBN: 978-1-4525-3557-9 (sc)
ISBN: 978-1-4525-3559-3 (hc)

Library of Congress Control Number: 2011909198

Printed in the United States of America

Balboa Press rev. date: 7/25/2011

Dedicated to you. May you find peace.

INTRODUCTION

It has been said that the only thing permanent in life is change. The types of change are as vast as the universe itself, from physical change as simple as getting a haircut to change on a cosmological scale such as the birth of a new star in the heavens. Is any one particular change more important than others? That is a question best left answered by every individual on a personal level, for a change that brings joy to one person may cause another to shrug their shoulders in indifference

The story in this book is one of change, a poetic journey of one souls trials of depression, paranoia and hopelessness to the awakening of hope and the inspiration found by a renewed love of life. The path of the story will be familiar to many, as I am not the only one who has walked it, but it is unique as all of our individual stories are.

If any reader sees a bit of themselves in my story, that surely is a good thing. The problems each of us face, real or imagined, as we trek through the years can be so similar it is a wonder we feel ashamed, guilty or angry about them. You can be sure many of the people you see each day are dealing with the same issues, the same headaches or the same heartaches as you are. Some of us find the strength to overcome and to learn from our past experiences, some of us continue in circles of self-destruction. My hope for this book is that some of you will use my words to find the strength to avoid becoming one of the latter.

Chapter 1

THE DESCENT

The events that can trigger an individuals descent into depression and hopelessness are unique to each of us. Where we can all find common ground is not in the specifics of the events, but in the generalities that are universally present in the human race, be it the death of a loved one, the break-up of a couple, childhood traumas, addiction to drugs or alcohol, terminal illness in oneself or others, a dream that can seemingly never be realized or a deep spiritual confusion, to name some of the triggers that come immediately to mind.

My own personal loss of hope began in my eighteenth year, though I did not see it at the time. It is an unfortunate truth that most of us cannot discern where our descent begins until we are able to detach ourselves from ourselves and look into our haunted pasts without a fog of denial and self-pity clouding our vision. To recognize that we ourselves are the cause of our own misery is too much for us to admit while in the throws of depression or addiction. We rather take on the role of "the victim" and everything negative that happens to us and those around us only serves to reinforce our misplaced view that the world or God himself is out to cause us as much pain as we can humanly endure before looking to self-annihilation as the only way to stop our suffering

Those of us who have considered ending our own lives or have attempted it and failed, may have foolishly and selfishly believed that the world and our loved ones would be better off without us. That others love us and are trying to pull us out of our self-created pit never occurs to us. Our fleeting moments of happiness only bring us more pain and our world becomes a living hell, a nightmarish landscape populated by demons and phantoms sent to torment us. Our despair and self-loathing becomes a vicious cycle and in a weird reversal of perception, we eventually begin to take a masochistic pleasure from our self-inflicted pain. It is only by an extreme act of will, the fortitude of others in their desire to help us, the healing flame of love, a joyful spiritual awakening, finding a religion that gives us peace of mind or the inexorable passage of time that causes us to wake from our zombie-like stupor and ghost-like non-existence and non-participation to the very real and very beautiful joys of life.

In my eighteenth year I did as many young men do and enlisted in the military. My extremely poor eyesight made me ineligible to become a soldier, an event I look upon favorably now but also with the realization that being told I was unfit to serve my country was the beginning of my disillusions concerning what I was told life after high-school was supposed to be like, the workings of the "system" and the American Dream in general. At the time I merely shrugged off this metaphorical slap in the face and went on to the reasonable back-up plan, which was leaving the confinement, comfort and security of home for the excitement and freedom of college. It was exactly that exhilarating experience of novelty and new found freedom from parental and high-school control systems that served to quicken my descent.

The next four years are when I began to express my hidden anguish and confusion in poetry. The exact details of those years are nowhere near as important as the inner roller-coaster of emotions and outer false front of forced smiles and bitter laughter. I will let the poetry speak for itself.

Labyrinth

Locked doors and cold walls,
Is what I see around me.
Someone let me in.
Dead end streets and cold heat,
A maze of ghostly haze.
I cannot get out.

Light of the Moon

By the light of the moon,
I wander in the outer lands.
The sun is too hot, too bright,
For me, a creature of the night.
Closing my diseased eyes,
I open my minds eye.
Walking backwards on the middle path,
To find the path in the night,
Am I wrong or in the right?
I am not a hypocrite,
I just change my mind,
Too fast for you
To help my mental health.
By the light of the moon,
I carelessly meditate.
It is then,
The worlds energy flow is low,
And so is mine.

Insomnia

A strange vision fades as I rise,
And see the blackness of the night.
Shadows dance upon the walls,
Haunting shapes of evil might.
A hood of darkness over my world,
The sun has gone beyond the moon.
Devils and demons are now at play,
And hounds of hell will howl soon.
The time of fear is nearly here,
I walk, I talk, but all for naught.
Things unseen I try to see,
As a smell of sweat stains the air.
Laughing, the ghost of memory appears,
And the odor of fear is everywhere.
The dream slows, my mind now alive,
Smoke a joint, drink a beer,
Some TV might be the thing,
Or a hot fire to melt my fear.
Tick tock, tick tock,
The clock loves to mock.
I think it better to mock the clock,
Tock tick, tock tick.
I grasp onto a flaming torch,
A book of truth to show the way.
The poems fill my eyes and ears,
With light as bright as day.
Page after page a war is fought,
The Shadow attacking verse of power,
Distraction now its only ally,
As the bard sings with dawns hour.
With words here and truth there,
The masters guide me from my chair.
The clash for the sky nears its end,
Another night in waking dreams,
Walking with those alive and dead,
Where everything is not as it seems.
Something is gained,
And something is lost,
The real is here and now I'm off,
Thinking again about what I lost.

Period

Remember when we met,
!!!
How innocent it was,
XOXOXOXO
What we learned,
!!?!!?!!?
Where it led,
XXX
Our love,
U&I
Our fall,
??!??!??!
Then you were gone,
^^ ^^ ^^

What happened,
?@##$%%!!$&**%$?
Now one thing remains,
???
I hope the pain ends soon
...

Ugly Inspiration

A little bit of this,
And a bottle full of that,
Until I am not quite sure,
Just when and where I'm at.
Seeing double, Seeing triple,
How low can I sink?
Again I've had too much to drink.
Call me a drunk,
I've heard it before,
It doesn't seem to bother,
This beautiful whore.
Blacking out, whiting in,
It all aids my pen.

That's Why

Walking down the street today,
There's people running everywhere,
A few smile or nod their heads,
Most glance and turn their eyes away.
What is it they see,
That turns their eyes from me?
That's why,
I pour my rage on the page,
Cause with my anger comes a danger,
Of losing all control.
Honesty and the Golden Rule,
Are being twisted to evil tools,
Insecurity and ignorance,
Used by power and money hungry fools.
Just remember when you die,
All you save is left behind.
That's why,
I lock the gate on my hate,
And watch it burn itself out,
Cause with my anger comes a danger,
Of losing all control.
That's why,
For me to write
Is to get through the night.
Even with my sorrow,
I can still change tomorrow,
By living today.

*I*f there is any rule about writers or poets critiquing their own work, well, I am about to break it. From my perspective, there is none better suited to the analysis of a written piece of work than the author. Of course, if all writers and poets did this, then the critics would all be looking for work elsewhere. To be fair, outside evaluation of any writing is needed as we all take something different away from the stories and poetry we read. Not to mention that the mystery surrounding writers and their work must be maintained at all costs.

That being said, my intent is to shed as much light as possible onto what my poetry meant for me at the time. By doing so I will hopefully allow the reader to see themselves in my words and to see that our problems, and joys, are only as large as we make them or only get as big as we allow them to.

Taking our attention back to the dark and dreary poetry of previous pages, it helps to understand that first and foremost, poetry is meant to be *felt*. No amount of left brain logical thought will ever connect anyone to a particular poem. A common experience or emotion, something we as the reader can relate to individually, is what brings poetry to life and gives it soul.

When I look back at those old haunted writings, I see a lost soul, someone lashing out at the world with written words. I also see fear, uncertainty and confusion. So how did I get to that point?

What made me feel like I was trapped in such a hopeless maze that seemed to be without an exit? The answer, as the truth usually is, is simple. I felt abandoned. The poem *Labyrinth* reflects my feelings of loneliness.

I was pretty upset with God back then and I released that anger in my 19th year by crying out for help in the most pathetic and selfish way possible. I cut my wrists. It was an infantile act, my inner child and inner tyrant crying out for attention. I wanted someone else to make it all better, never realizing until years later that ultimately the responsibility to heal my wounds was my own. The irony of the situation was that the two people that could help me the most were the ones I hated the most, namely God and myself.

After my childish tantrum with a razor, I took refuge in books, drugs and alcohol along with sporadic episodes of writing. I also spent a lot of time working on my hand - eye coordination by mashing buttons on video game controllers. All in all a very unhealthy lifestyle.

Sunlight became my enemy and I lived a kind of vampire – like existence, not really feeling energized until night. After sundown I began feeding my inner void with an assortment of drugs, alcohol and non – stop partying. Just an oversized kid playing with updated toys in a hopeless struggle to divert my attention away from my repressed problems. The poems *Light of the Moon* and *Insomnia* portray my alienation from the activities of the day.

To further complicate matters I was reading a lot of books about religion, spirituality and mysticism. I went through a quickly passing phase where the New/Old Age Wiccan religion became my thing. Then it was on to Zen Buddhism. My own particular flavor of Zen is more accurately described as "beat Zen", which doesn't even come close to what actual Buddhism is meant to be about. Shirking ones responsibilities with forced smiles and laughter while being tormented inside is not what I feel the Buddha and Bodhidharma had in mind.

There were a few times I actually managed to quiet my mind and enter what can rightly be meditation. Unfortunately these instances came about by sheer force of will rather than any feeling of inner calm. I had several spiritual experiences in my 20th year which I foolishly decided to tell a few people about. Paranoia overwhelmed me and I began to believe the world was out to get me (perhaps in a way the world is out to get all of us, not with malicious intent but with hard lessons).

I began to believe my life was hopeless and I began searching for the exit. Drugs, alcohol, paranoia, repressed anger and fear all came together in a negative zero-point. In my 21st year, I overdosed on prescription pills, took every pill in every bottle I could find in the house. I awoke four days later in a hospital feeling miserable and ashamed. I couldn't even kill myself successfully.

The next eight years were a see – saw roller coaster between zombie – like inactivity, drug and alcohol abuse and brief moments of lucidity in which I began to seek myself and ask questions about life, death and the world in general. Inner confusion and plenty of built up rage against myself and the world was my daily and nightly state of being, shown in the pieces *Period, Ugly Inspiration* and *That's Why*.

Chapter 2

THE BATTLE

For nearly eight years after my failed overdose I fought a long battle with myself. When I began to awaken from my self – induced coma of hatred and apathy toward everything, myself included, I saw the phrase "We are our own worst enemy." is a cliché and a truth for a reason. I was the enemy I was fighting with. The world and the people in it had nothing to do with my problems and if I would have just paid a bit more attention, I would have seen that both were trying with determination to make me realize that life was not as bad as I believed.

What is it about many of us that makes us search for something or someone to make it all better for us? We can search for doctors, counselors, psychiatrists, friends or lovers for many years, only to realize these people cannot help us unless we put in the effort to help ourselves. I do not believe we can connect with anyone until we first connect with who we really are inside. Until we manage to be truthful to ourselves and respect who we are, we will always be fighting tooth and nail against those we seek out for help.

My own inner struggle came out in the form of the eternal battle between good and evil. At least that is how I saw it for many years. Magnificent angels and devas wielding glowing swords of truth and justice doing battle against monstrous devils and demons encased in fiery auras was my view of light versus dark. My attraction toward books of heroic fantasy, violent video games and years of battling wicked monsters inside my head while playing pen and paper role-playing games had much to do with this I feel. Perhaps the human vision of the dualistic war between good and evil, God and the Devil or ignorance and knowledge may never fade completely away, but as for the inner battle it may be better to be a diplomat and make peace with Shadow aspects of ourselves..

Battle

The angels horn sings and battle begins,
An ancient war of angels and demons,
Brought about by ones betrayal.
As weapons clash we wonder who will last,
The Creator and the Enemy fight on,
With mortal caught in the chaos.
Fight for truth and you will see the proof,
How many more tears of pain and fear,
Must be shed before our suffering ends?
Revealed if you've had the revelation,
Pick you side and enjoy your ride,
For battle has been joined,
Coming soon to a head,
Fight on my friend,
For you will soon be dead.
Hell is here,
And death is near.
Revelations revealed,
The Apocalypse now.
In this life or the next,
When do you think will be best?
Evil is impatient,
But good is inherent.

Find the Dragon

Inside of you and me,
Is a beast we rarely see.
With scales of shimmering steel,
A strength not seeking to kneel.
Eyes that pierce the darkness,
Tongue that will never confess.
Find your dragon,
It has begun.
Breath made up of flame,
Brain bordering the insane.
Claws seeking to rend,
The evil, to Hell it will send.
Find your dragon,
It has begun.

Destination

Destination; Heaven,
A place lost to history,
Where we all can be free.
A garden smelling of wisdom,
A sun like a scintillating prism.
Violence and war lost to memory,
A place where we can simply be.
Destination; Hell
A place to house the wicked,
A place where the good are sickened.
A garden reeking of disease,
A sun meant to freeze.
Violence, a common affair,
Guns and knives brought to bear.
Destination; Earth,
A battleground made and set adrift,
Where through our dreams we sift.
A garden of Eden, evil, and ecstasy,
Amidst the commotion a soul sits, me.
Living the good life, fighting the good fight,
Trying hard to make sure we strive,
Toward what is left of right.

Before Me

The darkness I see when my eyes are blind,
Is still there when they're open wide.
Looking through a thunder cloud,
Afraid to stand, refusing to bow, .
Bend my knees, take me down,
To the ground, help me see,
What is before me.
The stench of fear is in the air,
It s only me, alone and scared.
Looking through a shimmering gloom,
What I see are scenes of doom,
Bend my knees, force me down,
To the ground, help me see,
What is before me.
Look towards the blackened sky,
And ask yourself what gets you by.
Still I stare into the void,
As my love starts to get annoyed.
Bend my knees, take me down,
To the ground, help me see,
What is before me.

It Hurts

My will has almost broken in two,
My soul a shadow,
My eyes always blue.
My curse is I see too much,
Of evil's work,
And it hurts.
Let God help me if he has the will,
Let him keep my wandering mind still.
My curse is I see to much,
Of evil's work,
And it hurts.
Heaven and Hell both beckon me in,
And I wonder if life is worth the sin.
But hope remains,
I know that now,
I simply must bend my head and bow.
My miracle is I see too much,
Of God's work,
And still it hurts.

To Get High

I love to get high,
On life,
And dream and fly.
In endless meditation,
On a certain situation,
On life,
On rebirth into another form.
Will I again be born,
Or will I get to rest?
Free from the material,
Able to focus on the spiritual.
To help my master in his quest,
To help him lay evil to rest.
Because I love to get high,
On life,
So until we achieve victory,
There will be no rest for me.

Light and Dark

Without the Dark there can be no Light,
But the more we ignore the suffering we see,
Deeper and Darker the Night will be.

Release

Chaos and pain,
Disease and rain.
This is what I know,
They release the word flow.
Beginning and End,
Enemy and Friend.
They are one and the same,
Just with different names.
Yin and Yang,
Happiness and Shame.
Release your guilty past,
And let all your pain pass

Light We Share

Walk with me,
And talk with me.
Do you believe in me,
Or is it too hard to see?
The light we share,
Must be brought to bear.
If we are to live in better days,
We must learn to drop to our knees and pray.
The light we share,
Must soon be brought to bear.

Anarchy

If chaos reigned supreme,
Where would we go to dream?
If love was gone,
Hate would be a song.
His plan must be stopped,
Or our world will be lost,
To Anarchy.
Lust and Greed are his tools,
Embraced by many, the fools.
Will Sloth and Envy be the new ideals,
Or will someone somewhere make an appeal?
Will the Wrath of our pride bring us down,
Will Gluttony make us all look like clowns?
Suffering will make us its slaves,
Unless the good can be brave.
Find the good in yourself,
And share it with someone else.
Then we can begin anew,
And Anarchy will be eschew.

As is evident in the poems *Victim, Battle, Find the Dragon* and *Destination,* I had a vision of life that was apocalyptic in the extreme. Everything and everyone in the world was placed neatly on either the side of good or evil. The "us or them" mentality. Neutrality and balance did not exist for me, war was the solution and I was the hero.

Thinking back, imagining myself in the role of the hero was one the main reasons I kept on getting out of bed in the morning (or afternoon, sad but true). The protagonist in a story never gives up, no matter what the world throws at them. This self-centered delusion of mine, combined with an inherent stubbornness, eventually became a saving grace and allowed me to take better notice of other people. Now, I am beginning to see that everyone is the hero of their own life story and one of the jobs of those closest to us is to help us better ourselves, sometimes even with pain, tough love and outright lies.

Personally, I feel that lying and telling someone what they *want* to hear is the worst way to offer assistance, but that's just me. Getting straight to the heart of the matter, without any candy flavored coating, can break through the strongest emotional or mental wall any of us can put up to defend our self-image. The brutal truth, whether we find it inside ourselves and have the courage to accept it or it is told to us by a well-meaning and compassionate friend, is always the slap in the face needed to wake us up. Lies just will not cut it when dealing with the healing of the heart and soul.

In the battle to find my own heart and soul, I often felt like a puppet that was being manipulated by forces beyond my control. Paranoia combined with drug and alcohol abuse did not help this feeling, as shown in the piece *Before Me.*

During this time of my life, I did not believe I had free will. Every situation and every interaction with other people was a trap and I was the target. I truly believed this and still have those feelings occasionally today. My only defense was solitude, losing myself in drugs and alcohol or living vicariously through movies and video games. I became very proficient at being emotionless and seeing every life situation as a battle to be won. In my mind, I won every battle and I was always right. Hindsight being as it is, I realize I missed out on a lot of good things with my dark versus light mentality. And I was wrong more often than I like to admit.

The remainder of the poems show hints of sunlight peeking through the storm clouds. No matter how long our dark night of the soul is, we occasionally see brief flashes of the day. These too fleeting glimpses help us keep wading through the mud and the muck of our own misery. They are hope amid hopelessness, beckoning us to smile, laugh and realize the world is only as bad as we make it.

Chapter 3

LIMBO

At the same time I was warring with myself and others, today I recognize I had put myself in a kind of limbo, a self-created purgatory. When I say limbo, I mean a place where everything is static and colors exist in only shades of gray. Every day is the same and any accomplishments are quickly rubbed out by bouts of depression or drowned in pints of beer. It is a very sad and dreary place to be.

Despite the hopelessness I felt while in limbo, I met some great people there. Friends I see now that were trying to help me escape and to give me the comfort of their presence. Perhaps some of those people were (or are) undercover angels. Probably some of the relationships I had in limbo were of the selfish, misery loves company kind also. I know there was plenty of misery inside me to go around, so I am guilty of that as well.

There was also plenty or raucous laughter, rambling conversions about pretty much everything while in a fog of smoke, painful shots of burning liquor of all types and many nights spent in the embrace of music spanning many generations. Wasted youth or valuable learning experience? Again, probably a lot of both.

Limbo was where I discovered how much self torture I could inflict and how much pain and anger I could bottle up. Luckily, I found the doorway out before I either imploded or exploded. I may not be all the way through the door yet, I can still feel the void trying to suck me back in occasionally, but I have enough of myself across the threshold where I can take the time to appreciate this life, the world and the people in it.

Freeing oneself from limbo is not easy, but it can be done by gritting our teeth, focusing our attention on bettering ourselves and those around us and by humbling our pride and asking someone for a little help. For whatever reason, there always seems to be people out there who have more faith in us than we do in ourselves. We need to be grateful for those giving souls and show them our appreciation from time to time.

All Night

Staying up all night,
Sometimes makes me uptight.
Is it the darkness,
Or the silence,
That disturbs me?
Sometime the drugs says it's alright,
For me to stay up all night.
Sometimes it's the dreams I receive,
The ones where I always bleed,
That disturbs me.
If you stay up all night too,
Know someone in the world,
May be staying up with you.

Sidewinder

A sidewinder,
Between good and evil.
The line is stretched thin,
On either side.
The road to goodness,
Is marked by hardship,
For evil by far,
Is the easy way out.

The Projection

Relax,
All of you,
Mind awake,
Body asleep,
That is where we need to be.
Vertigo,
Fall in to sleep,
Cut the strings,
All but one,
And your body is gone.
Your spirit is free,
Flying around,
On a nameless plane,
No arms,
No legs,
Just the eye.
Not to look,
But to see,
Everything we could be.

Unreality

The human mind is a fascinating construct,
It is all any of us have to work with.
Every fleeting second of each passing day,
We explore a little more of that vast space,
Inside of our seemingly endless brain.
As we live we can see how subjective,
How fragile,
The reality we take for granted can be.
And when the unreal becomes real,
In anyone's eyes,
Can it still be called unreal?

Knowledge

My reality is for me,
As yours is for you.
Our every judgment hangs,
On the brink of error.
Knowledge is an unending journey,
At the edge of uncertainty.
What you know in one world,
Could be useless in another.

Nothing

I am nothing,
I have no eyes,
But still I can see.
I have no ears,
But still I hear the words,
I have no arms,
But still my fists are clenched.
I have no legs,
But still I can run.
I have no wings,
But still I can fly.
I am nothing,
I am everything.

Everything

Inside, Outside,
Devoid of definition.
Thoughts, Emotions,
There is a perfect explanation.
Everything I was,
Everything I am,
Everything I will be,
Changes, Spiraling,
In constant fluctuation.
To be, not to be,
Always our decision.

The Middle Path

This is where I leave,
This is where I get off.
On a train of much middle,
My end is my beginning,
And forever is in between.
This is how I live,
This is how I get off.
In a car with the crazies,
Eye open with eyes closed,
Staying near to those who know,
A long time spent,
In the middle of the road.

Clay

We all have a disguise,
Created by our mind.
The cover of our spirit,
But right now I need it.
To learn and to explore,
What all of this is for.

Birth to Rebirth

I'm singing in the rain,
Running from the pain.
I love the thunder,
And the lightning.
They keep me from fighting,
With things thought left behind.
What pursues me is what,
Experience has shown me.
I forge on with the years,
I have left before death,
In search for the Truth,
Of infinite youth.

*D*espite the unchanging nature of any of our own personal limbos, or perhaps because of it, it is a decent place to do some philosophizing about the nature of reality. I spent far too much time thinking about things that may not be all that important. One thing I am sure of is while in limbo, I never had any real sort of personal identity. I was nothing and everything, a mimic devoid of my real personality. There were no life goals, no moments to look forward to with excitement and personal growth took place at a snails pace. If life is like a highway, then I was sleeping in my car at a rest stop.

The poetry in this chapter needs no explanation. I was searching for an identity while letting the world bat me around like a man-sized pinball. If there was a silver lining to my stay in limbo, it was the people that I met there and the fact that I actually *was* beginning to seek out my true self.

Chapter 4

THE SYSTEM

*D*uring my years of depression, I occasionally poked my head up from the hibernation hole I had dug for myself and took a suspicious glance at events unfolding in the world. These apathetic moments only made me more miserable, as I saw only the negative side of society. War, terrorism, poverty and disasters of all kinds swirled around the edges of my vision in a maelstrom of chaos. Never once did I think that I intentionally sought out events of fear and violence to feed the void inside of myself. I saw no hope for myself and therefore saw no hope for the world.

In my poetry, I began taking potshots at a system I rarely participated in and indeed, was helping me to get by.. My targets were television, the American Dream, representative democracy, greed and war. Even to this day, I am not altogether fond of any of the above, although I see now that the American Dream is whatever we want it or need it to be.

Having been a child who spent countless hours staring into television sets watching sitcoms, family dramas, science fiction programs, police dramas, cartoons and playing video games, there is a chance that too much television could be harmful. It did mine in any case and I now avoid television with a focused determination. I have done enough vicarious living to last several lifetimes. If you enjoy television, then laugh, cry, sigh and smile to your hearts content, but this soul has filled his cup to the brim with fictional stories and is still trying to empty it out.

I once thought the American Dream was one of fame and fortune, living the rock star lifestyle. For some of us maybe that is true, but what about the rest of us with simpler tastes? How about being in a comfortable space surrounded by family and friends and finding a community in which we can be a part of? A place where we feel we belong, a home. Perhaps the feeling of being at home is the sensation most of us are seeking and maybe we all need to flail around blindly in darkness for a time before finding our own unique niche. Hopefully the stumbling blocks, pit traps and snares on your road to where you feel you belong do not keep you down for as long a time as they did for myself.

If one the traps laid to snatch you up into endless debate about who is right and who is wrong is politics, well, I can only say good luck to you. In that circus, everyone is trying to be the strongman (or woman) and anyone who disagrees is asking to be one of the barbells he throws around.

As for greed and war, I feel there is too much of both floating around these days, Is peace and prosperity really achieved with machine guns and bombs? Sure, many nations and empires are built on war and conquest and supporting the troops is considered patriotic, but is it written down anywhere that peace is *not* patriotic? Is there a law against wanting violence and war to end? Do *you* want our men and women of any nation to keep dying in war or do *you* want them to come home for good? There is no middle ground with that question. Where do *you* stand?

Preacher

Opposites will interact,
Counterbalance, Counteract.
The yin and yang,
A season of change,
The balance is broken,
It no longer functions.
The world is at an impasse,
Everything going too fast,
As many deceivers as teachers.
Tonight at ten,
We feature the preacher,
Everyone is down on their knees,
Worshiping their TV.
TV!
What is it we need?
TV!
What do we believe?
Hear me when I say,
Find your own way,
The TV may be stealing our souls away.
Find your own way.

Stranger

Destroy one to raise another,
Might seem right until you're the other.
One mind right, all others wrong,
Pick and choose the ones that belong,
To perhaps live in fear because of your beliefs,
All because you may be a stranger to the chief.

Syndication

This is life,
Work and play,
Day by day,
Stuck in a routine,
It's all a bad dream.
This is life,
A husband, A wife,
A house, A car,
You've made it far,
Haven't you?

The Dream

The American Dream,
Is not what it seems,
You're a prisoner of a system,
That's slowly falling down.
I take a look around,
This is what I see,
Millions of failed seekers,
Trapped in their normalcy.
It's sad to bring it out,
But one of them is me,
Trying to find a way through,
The lies of this human zoo,
The mis-directions of this circus,
Can you see it too?
The winds of change are blowing,
A storm is taking form.

Iron, Steel, Blood and Tears

The club, the hammer, the mace, the ax,
Let us create to destroy.
The sword, the spear, the dagger, the dirk,
The world is our toy.
The sling, the stone, the bow, the arrow,
War creates, doesn't it?
The crossbow, the cannon, the musket, the pistol,
Let's do it for the fun of it!
Machine guns, missiles, tanks and torpedoes,
What's yours is mine, what's mine is mine.
Jets, bombers, subs and stealth,
Now we can kill at anytime!
Atom, Hydrogen and Neutron bombs,
Isn't it great, can't you see?
Hiroshima, Nagasaki,
Stop the violence,
Let us be free.

*A*ll of the poems written in this chapter were completed after the terrible events of 9/11. Like so many of us, I was glued to the television for many days after. It was during this period of time I began to realize how flooded with violence, fear-mongering and dogmatic preaching our boxes of entertainment are filled with. These things were all there before, or course, but I began to be consciously aware of them after 9/11.

My only defense against the constant barrage of fear, hate and thinly veiled prejudice coming from the television was to dump my frustrations onto the page. *Preacher* was my silent cry to the people of the world to think for themselves and not base their opinions on what they heard on the television or read in the news. Rarely do those mediums give us the whole story as is seen from *both* sides of any event or argument.

We would do well to remember that those whose beliefs, customs, clothing, language and lifestyle differ from ours are human beings also. They have thoughts and feelings much like our own. They are not strangers or enemies, they are simply people we have not gotten to know or understand *yet*. Is America the best country in the world or is it *a* country *of* the world? We are supposed to be the melting pot, a haven of freedom and choice open to all colors and creeds. Perhaps we should start acting like it and try to coexist without violence or prejudice. And maybe, just maybe, the rest of the world is waiting for us to set an example.

Chapter 5

QUESTIONS

When we embark upon the long and sometimes terrifying road to find our true selves, we inevitably ask a goodly amount of questions about a variety of topics. Asking a question is the easy part, it is finding an answer within ourselves without the aid of books or other people's perceptions that puts the word "quest" in question. Seeking answers about who we really are and what we believe to be true is a journey we all must take alone. Our friends, family and sometimes random strangers can give us encouragement, advice or occasionally make our trek a bit harder, but only we ourselves can walk our inner roads.

Perhaps the most difficult questions we can ask ourselves have to do with death and the afterlife. Is death an ending, a new beginning or both? Does the human soul continue on in a non-physical nature after the death of the body? Is there an afterlife and if so, what is it like? I struggled with questions like these for many years before coming to my own personal conclusions. I believe in the existence of the soul because I sometimes can *feel* it. The only words to explain this feeling are "inner peace", something which each of us has our own definition for. If you can feel your own soul then there must be something decent waiting after death.

Confusion

A boy and a man,
I wish I knew,
Just who I am.
Eighteen, ninety one,
When exactly do we,
Have to stop having fun?

Seeking

Am I a seeker of the Way,
Or a seeker of a way?
A Way of spiritual growth,
Where sits material wealth?
A seeker on the Way,
Or a seeker on my way?
Either way it is perfectly clear,
The paradox of why I am here.

Look

Look at me,
What do you see?
Look me in the eyes,
With these eyes I cry.
Look at me,
What do you see?
Look me in the face,
Can you see my disgrace?
Look at you, Can you?
Look in your eyes,
You cry with those eyes.
Look at you, Will you?
Look in your own face,
Are you a disgrace?

An End

If you knew in absolute truth,
That tomorrow your world would end,
Tell me, what would you do?
Riot, loot, drugs, booze,
Spend time with your family,
Or forget them entirely?
Seek out a long lost love,
Or give in to a primal lust?
In an end becomes clear,
Can you face it without fear?

Bliss

How long can you exist in a state of bliss?
The thirst to know the reasons why,
Will always be there with us,
As we struggle to survive.
How long can you exist in a state of bliss?
To be a bit discontent drives the mind,
Seeking the unknown and the new,
Searching for ways to help the blind.
How long can you exist in a state of bliss?
Do you notice the suffering around you,
Don't you get pissed,
Do thoughts fly so fast you have to cease and desist?
How long can you exist in a state of bliss?
The need to move on and see what is next,
Is constantly with me,
Keeping me vexed.
How long can you exist in a state a bliss?

Chapter 6

PERCEPTIONS

What is perception? Is it what our five senses tell us? I feel that is a part of it, but perhaps perception has more to do with how we relate to our surroundings and our own thoughts and emotions toward others. Does consciously thinking positive thoughts improve our mood and our relationships with the people we interact with? Do we, if fact, create our own realities based upon what we think, feel and dream about? If today's reality is created by yesterdays thoughts, do we actually wake up each morning in a slightly altered universe?

I pondered these questions many a night in my search for the truth about myself and the world around me. Now that I no longer have the haze of addiction and self-pity clouding my vision I see the thing about the truth is that everyone has their own version of it. What is true to you may not be true to me. Is that what the phrase, "To each their own," refers to? That the truth is completely relative to the individual? Is their one universal truth? Is life really, my story, your story and the truth?

The conclusion I have reached about perception and truth is that to find truth, we must learn to be ourselves, open, honestly and without shame. When we begin to live a life that is true to who we are and what we choose to believe in, I feel it is then that our perception can be changed toward the positive. The meaning of life for me is to find something that makes you happy and stick with it. Be it family, friends, lovers, reading, writing, sports, TV, camping, farming, gardening, hunting or a countless number of other activities we can enjoy. If you take joy in something then do it and do it with all your heart and do it well.

I have realized only just recently that many of us shy away from the things that make us the happiest. We could look at why some of us do this and say that only suffering and hardship make us better people. The harder the fall or the more crushing the defeat then the larger the gain in the future. Happiness is relegated to something that is only achievable at some far off hypothetical moment in the future. Well, I say is there any reason it can't be both? Should we just suffer and grin and bear it, waiting for a future moment that may never come? Is there any law about truly feeling happy for a part of a certain day and suffering during a different part?

A good example is does someone who works hard to save up enough money to buy a new car enjoy the time when they are working toward that new purchase or do they only allow themselves to feel satisfaction and enjoyment when the new car finally is theirs? The novelty quickly wears off on a new car. The grumbling about payments, insurance, gas mileage, repairs and maintenance soon begins. We probably have all done this ourselves or know someone who has.

So what is it that most of us seem to be striving for, that future moment when everything is okay and we can stop tormenting ourselves? I feel it is the search for happiness, the warm feeling of being at home, that drives us to endure so much self-inflicted misery. Maybe that feeling is always with us, but we choose to distract ourselves from it because we have a strange sense we aren't worthy of it. I believe we are all worthy of that feeling. We just have to stop and choose to live in that feeling. Happiness is here, now at this very moment. So why not embrace it with a smile?

Perceptions: Ignorance and Sin

The Scavengers of Time,
With evil eyes intent on the herd,
Searching for those weak and wounded,
And the ones lost and in despair.
Dirty claws reeking of disease and death,
Inflict festering wounds with sharp precision,
Even cut and bleeding the strong endure,
With power and speed of mind they seek,
Enlightenment for the ignorance within,
Salvation for the sins without.

Perceptions: Zen

Blinking, I brush my mind clean,
From the trappings of all the teaching I have seen.
Briefly, I wonder why I wasted time in such useless thought,
When a rock lying in the sand is what I truly sought.
But then that thought is swiftly swept away,
By a bird flying by the sun on this special day.
The sound of one hand clapping for a while puzzled me,
Until I caught a fleeting glimpse of what we all could be.
Now instead of a mirror, I see things through a window,
No reflection or interpretation,
Just simple observation.

Perceptions: Friends

Do you see me as I am,
Or how you think I should be?
Sometimes it is hard to tell.
You certainly are unique,
Maybe it's the way you speak,
Always quick to hold me end up,
If my lips cannot find the words.
Your presence feels of family,
A comfortable kindred spirit,
With me now as I sit.
And to something I once asked you,
An answer I think I found,
Perceptions of truth, this life,
And living to find a dream.
Even not knowing the dream we seek,
We go on, at times strong, at times weak,
Step into my shoes, my friend,
See me as I see you,
And I'll see me as you do.

Take a Look

Take a look outside as the world revolves,
And see for yourself our lost resolve.
It seems our philosophy on technology,
Is slowly destroying our decency.
Just think in about twenty years,
This place we all call a home,
Could be a breeding ground for human clones.
Take a look at what pushes my pen, my friend,
And you ll see that I too wished for the end.
With a whole lot of pride and nothing left to hide,
I write this rhyme to try and help the blind.
This is for those that are scared of their fate,
And for the ones that can't wait to see the gate.
In a dream I've seen how the world will scream,
If we don't unite to fight for what is left of right,
And to protect and preserve our way of life.
Take a closer look at why I write this rhyme,
And you'll see that we might be running out of time.
Because our love for hate must be put away,
If we wish to live in better days.
It's the conflict of the human race,
The one that we fight day to day.
It's a shame to see that the ignorant way,
Is what taught a lot of people how and what to say.
I know you know what I mean and that you've seen that scene.
And I can relate because I've had some falls,
The insults they throw to try and make me fall,
It would take the rest of the day to recite them all.
And when the wheel of time says it's my time to shine,
You ll see a gleam in my eye because I've learned to fly.
Take a look outside as the world revolves,
And take a closer one as we all evolve.

Sleep

To slumber and to dream,
Where all is not as it seems.
Dark for some,
Light for others,
Our thoughts, sleep smothers.
Confused, Chaotic,
Wonderful, Pure,
Into its embrace we all are lured.
So go to sleep,
And count the sheep.
When you wake and yawn,
A new day will **dawn**.

Silence

The ability to speak,
Makes us humans unique.
But the power of silence,
Is more precious than diamonds.

You

You are the perfect inspiration,
The maker of our civilization.
It's comforting to know you're there,
Wise, compassionate,
Always aware.
I love because of you,
I'm always blue because of you.
You make me whole,
Complete my spirit.
You should know,
Right now I need it.
Your love and your mercy,
They make the good great,
And make evil shake.
Someday we will meet,
In spirit form I will greet,
You.

Just a Thought

To teach is to be taught,
A comforting thought.
Increase what you know,
And help others grow.

Airplane

The fast lane is like,
Life in an airplane,
Never knowing when,
The fuel is going to end.

The Beastman

Living for bodily passions,
And experiences of the flesh,
The Beastman is nearly mindless,
Full of adrenaline and zest.
Always searching for excitement,
Thrills,chills and danger,
Feeding an endless emotional hunger,
To greed and lust he is no stranger.
Extreme highs and lows,
Are his roadworthy companions,
With a gas tank near empty,
Secretly yearning for completion.

The Thinker

Sitting alone and wondering,
The Thinker is **her** name,
Problem solving and mental abstractions
Are **her** favorite games.
Knowing nothing of spirit,
The body **she** cares not for,
Seeking God is for others,
Physical sensations are a bore.
Pondering endless questions,
Answers **she** is looking to find,
Love and companionship **she** knows not,
Thirsting only for knowledge is **her** crime.

The Fairy

Living in a fantasy-land,
Is where the Fairy spends **her** time,
Fluttering this way and that,
Eyes fixed on the sublime.
Thoughts a maelstrom of color,
Body left far behind,
Dancing only with spirit,
The gods **she** is looking to find.
Carelessly helping and hurting,
Never stopping, never motionless,
Always laughing and loving,
In an endless spiritual bliss.

The Scientist

Figuring out how things work,
Be they of body or mind,
Making new combinations from old,
Is the Scientists idea of a good time.
Experimenting and analyzing,
Hypothesizing and theorizing,
His results can be helpful,
Or can end up terrorizing.
He feels and he thinks,
Adventures and creates,
But in the aspects of spirit,
He shies away from debate.

The Warrior

Made of muscle and passion,
With an unconquered spirit,
The Warrior lives without fear,
Her unthinking nature will not have it.
Living on instinct and energy,
Adventure calls her name,
Her decisions rash and reckless,
Lack of thought is to blame.
Brimming with life and with love,
Containing not so subtle hints of danger,
A loyal and steadfast companion,
If you make friends with **her** anger.

The Wizard

Possessing lightning quick thought,
And endless energy of spirit,
The Wizard walks through the land,
Healing those who live in it.
Solving problems as he goes,
Leaving riddles in his wake,
With intent to leave you wondering,
Hoping your spirit will awake.
Having a body that is often frail,
Sometimes smoking on a pipe,
The Wizard is destroying and creating,
Bringing the age of magic to life.

The Avatar

A being in perfect balance,
With a little less dark than light,
The Avatar befriended his Shadow,
Rendered it unable to fight.
Paying **attention** to his body,
Satisfying its **needs**,
With a mind put at peace,
And a spirit meant to lead.
Sacrificing destruction for creation,
The Avatar enjoys all of life,
He heals **without** hurting,
Being done with all strife.

*S*ubjects like time, memory, dreams, knowledge, God, ourselves and the world around us are all perceptions that are unique to us as individuals. Many of us share the same viewpoints about the above topics by way of religion, spirituality, science, psychology and shared experiences. The more of us who believe a thing is this way or that gives that particular perception strength, added force to bludgeon those of us who stand somewhere in the middle into believing one view is more right, or less wrong, than the others.

I believe the strength, or force, of any teaching lies not in how true it is, but in how much pressure is put upon people to conform through various means such as such as childhood indoctrination, peer pressure or societal "norms". In my experiences I have discovered that thinking and feeling for ourselves is the best course of action when deciding upon what we believe to be true. In other words, don't believe in something just because someone else told you to. The truth is inside of each of us.

While musing about psychology and metaphysics, I decided to invent a new approach to personality patterns in people. Instead of introverted, extroverted, feeling, thinking, id, ego and so on and so forth I based my classifications on three things; body, mind and spirit. The poems *The Beastman, The Thinker, The Fairy, The Scientist, The Warrior, The Wizard* and *The Avatar* is what I came up with. Since I see life as being something magical, all contain a touch of the mysterious and fantastic.

If you like the categories I created and see yourself as being a part of one, excellent! If they are too "out there" for you, well, that's okay too. It's your perception of the world that counts, not mine.

Chapter 7

WRITING

When I began to take the first tentative step out of my self-imposed exile from limbo, the realization that my infrequent bursts of creative writing had much to do with my survival therein. The blank page is where I vented and released tremendous amounts of stored up anger, anxiety, fear, personal problems, questions and the occasional bit of happiness. Writing was my salvation from the dark side of myself.

Getting rid of excess energy and stress is a much more important activity than I ever could have guessed. Sitting around drinking, smoking, playing video games and watching movies is a great way to repress your problems, but I do not recommend it for years at a time unless you also have a great way of releasing the built up negative energy on a day to day basis. So find an outlet for your problems, be it exercise, sports, physical labor or mental labor like creative writing, journal entries or puzzle solving. It could save your life.

The Fear

This right here is what I fear,
To bring my writing to bear,
Attempting to make my words clear,
This is constantly on my mind.
Going in circles around my work,
Good, bad, professional, amateur,
Would anyone tell me I can't right?
I hope they would,
Truth is good,
Will praise be well taken,
Or just inflate my ego?
But either way,
One thing endures,
My love goes into my work,
To write is the great redeemer,
For my soul.

Energy

I ate a lightning bolt today,
My energy was dangerously low.
Thunder is beginning in my head,
Turning slowly to a drum roll.
After the drums die my body vibrates,
With energy.
Shaken up, I get up,
Thinking what to do.
My notebook, my pen,
My salvation is here,
But so is television,
Computers and beer.

What Words Can Do

Written or spoken,
Our words have effect.
They can uplift our spirit,
Inspire our souls,
Take down our defenses,
Bring us in from the cold.
Though they are unable to break our bones,
They can damage our hearts,
So try to think before using them,
And you will stay out of the dark.

Seconds

This way and that way,
Why don't you just go away,
I am not blind to the signs,
So quit wasting my time.
Every second is precious,
And I relish being here,
In the present,
But the past is insistent,
Pressuring, Persistent.
The intrusions and delusions,
They cripple my creations,
With a strain and an energy drain,
That memory,
Has scarred upon my brain.
But even so,
Every second is golden,
And I love to bathe in the light,
Of the perfect inspiration,
That fuels my pen.

Creation

If you say I have a god complex,
I'll say you're right,
Because creation is in our nature,
Be it by heart, hand, mic or paper.
Give me a pen and I'll give you some lines,
Those lines might rhyme if it's worth my time,
Give you back a design of a mind,
That is so sublime,
You will have to,
Unwind, rewind, repeat and redesign,
Your own mind,
Just to figure out the sign.
The use of creation is what drives a nation,
Be it America, Europe, Africa or Asia.
We're all a part of the human race,
So wipe that look of superiority off your face,
Because we're made the same and we'll die the same,
But until I go I'll continue to create,
And play my part in the Cosmic game.

Salvage

When I feel a little rage,
I break fast for the page,
To turn my hate into fate.
I am good at burning the oil,
Spewing fire at my unwanted foil,
To make clear my vision is clean.
With my pen,
I do all that I can,
To salvage my soul,
The best that I can.

End to Begin

As I look to the page
I feel my mind engage,
Chaos turns to order
My thoughts start to turn over.
As I reach towards my pen
My spirit awakens within,
The devil falls off my shoulder,
And the angel takes over.
As I hold onto a sword of truth,
Muscles relax and nerves are soothed.
Intuition, Intellect and Sensation come together,
As the Unification is now over.
Mind, Body and Spirit now one,
Combined, more powerful than any gun.
My void beckons, I happily fly in,
As words of inner revelation begin.
No sights, no sounds, just musical silence,
A tune I transform,
Into a perfect confidence.
The pen is **like** iron,
The **blank page like a** magnet,
With a dream to create,
Something none will forget.

Writing to the Stars

Alone I sit here bleeding,
Thoughts from my head,
Chaos makes way for order,
The release of things unsaid.
Come here for a second,
And look to my mind,
Do you see the truth within,
Or are you too flying blind?
The blank page is where I find,
Freedom for my mind,
Expression of thought,
Cannot be bought,
It only can be sought.
I wish I may,
I wish I might,
Find the word,
That fits just right.
My pen is the comfort,
Of a thousand dreamless nights,
It often lulls me fast to sleep,
And protects me with its might.
Happy, sad, excited, mad,
What emotions do you like?
The choice is always yours,
Will it be the sprint,
Or will it be the hike?
The blank page is where I find,
The freedom of loves caress,
Many a sweet thing,
Can writing bring,
To those who start with nothing.
I wish I may,
I wish I might,
Find the way,
To write it right.

he poem, *The Fear,* displays the strange discomfort I often felt when trying to write while in limbo. This fear goes back to the odd behavior (at least for myself) of shying away from the activities that bring us the most joy. It could just be that while in a state of depression and hopelessness we do not feel *worthy* of any good feelings. Unless you count being on drugs, (and disconnected) almost everyday while waking up feeling like crap every morning a good feeling. I no longer do.

Seconds describes how a large part of my former miserable existence had to do with being stuck in the past, reliving old moments of regret, fear, paranoia and anxiety on a day to day basis. My constant negative state of mind on any given day made sure the next day was equally traumatizing.

I was at the height of my undeserved arrogance when I wrote the piece, *Creation.* I am more than a little ashamed of this poem, but I do still feel we as human beings are each meant to create something in our lives. Creating something that is uniquely our own can be a source of great happiness, the children of the world is a perfect example of this.

The poems *End to Begin* and *Writing to the Stars* are two of my favorite writing creations. I find peace of mind and inner happiness during the time I spend with my notebook and pen or my word processor. I may never create something none will forget or find the way to write it right every time, but I try my best on every page and in every poem.

Chapter 8

LOOKING UP

*I*f the world and your own troubles have you feeling down and out, be assured that when your clouds break, the sun will never look brighter or more beautiful. Finding hope when all seems lost is one of the best presents you can give yourself. It may take some time and some work, but the results will speak for themselves. If you never give up on yourself, you will find that no one will give up on you either.

Iron Soul

High and low,
Iron skin and iron soul.
I can't begin to explain,
How I was saved from the insane.
Questions asked,
Answers received.
Dark was my plight,
But saved by the light.
So I forge on ahead,
With a heart that's been bled.
Balance sought,
Balance earned.
High and low,
Iron skin and iron soul.

Suicide Risk

Once I was a suicide risk,
Go ahead, stare,
Come closer if you dare.
See the scars on my wrist,
That's none of your business.
Twice I was a suicide risk,
Depression and compulsion,
Created an obsession with addiction.
Grab onto a bottle, give the top a twist,
The rest is none of your business.
Thrice is never a charm,
If you seek to do harm,
So you should just drop it,
And stop talking about it,
Because the light in my mind,
Was so hard to find.
Now through the darkness I see,
Exactly where I want to be,
Without fear of spiritual entropy.

Divine

Here are some words,
To adhere to your ears,
Like a gift from an old seer.
Catch them quick on this page,
Before I send them back to my mental cage.
At the point of my pen,
I have a point to pen,
No erasers here,
Not in Zen.
Take a breath and calm your nerves,
Nothing here will be new news,
If you wonder what tomorrow will bring,
Trying to steer clear of what you fear,
Afraid of a boogeyman's sneer.
Tears of confusion,
Amidst a resolution,
Right in front of you is the solution.
Snap, crackle, pop you in the brain,
Your truth is in there somewhere,
Finding and bringing it to bear is rare.
Search your soul for all that is good,
And let it show,
As it should.
Negativity,
The worlds great destroyer,
Snap out of your depression and anger,
And the new you might seem like a stranger.
If you let your better half shine,
Then that is what should be called divine.

The Climb

Make up a rhyme and get free,
Is what someone once told me.
Now I can't recall,
If it was true or false.
When I started penning poems,
It was all uphill,
A long haul to the top.
We all need to stop,
Every once in a while,
To pump in some gas.
And check on our oil.
Then keep on trucking,
When I reach my top,
I'll look down and sigh,
Then help others up,
And teach them all how to fly.

Faith

Faith,
The belief without seeing,
To help us define our existence,
Our purpose.
To put trust in the unknowable,
But if we believe in the unseen,
Does that not make it visible,
In our hearts and in our souls?

Direction

Which direction do I choose,
That will bring me something new?
Is it up, down, left right times two,
All of them at once,
Or inward to the heart?
With all eight directions open to me,
And the intuitive knowledge of where I should be,
So whichever way my wind blows,
I'll jump on my carpet and just let go,
Without resisting what I am fated to see,
A balance created with the dark side of me.

Tree

I am now like a tree,
With roots deep and strong.
Do you see it in me,
Or are you still asleep?
Branches reaching out,
Seeking the sun.
Are you still in doubt,
That being like a tree can be fun?
Leaves green and beautiful,
Fed by a quiet rainstorm.
Is this way suitable,
Or too far from the norm?
Quiet, content, and at peace,
With birds singing all around.
I hope this feeling will never cease.

What Path?

What path is right for you,
Christian, Muslim, Buddhist, or Jew?
We all embrace a common cause,
Does that surprise or make you pause?
The choice is difficult and hard to trust,
But God has faith is each of us.
So follow the path that feels right for you,
Begin walking it,
And God will receive you.

Light

The light in my mind,
Was so hard to find.
I waded through what I had learned,
Over and over,
But that never brought me closer to right.
Ignorance and hate,
Could be your fate.
It was nearly mine.

Beauty

I saw Beauty today,
She was sitting quietly.
Dreaming, Thinking,
Being, Beautiful.
I admit I stared,
Perhaps a bit too long,
Hoping, Wishing,
Wanting, Love.

Words of Romance

Bolts of lightning embrace at the eyes,
In a union of spirit it is alright to cry,
Tears of bliss and happiness.
A lovers kiss is like candy for the soul,
Done just right it is pure delight,
Never growing old.
The curve of a neck or the swell of a breast,
Will always tremble under true loves caress.

Simple Words

To live is to love,
And to love is to live,
But which comes first?
Many times I have lived,
Surely I have loved,
Until I almost burst.
Love is always beauty,
And beauty lies within,
Our souls and our hearts.
So find something of beauty,
Inside or out,
That overflows with life,
It is **there** love will start.

Instant Karma

Give little concern,
About the written word.
The Way is never found,
In the language of letters,
You receive when you give,
A universal truth,
Instant karma,
For old and for youth.

Fresh Air

Smell of fresh air,
Free, without cares.
The leaf, the breeze,
The flower, the tree,
A moment of peace,
Content and at ease.
Time is just a word,
I wish I never heard,
Measures are without meaning,
They are forever changing,
But the smell of fresh air,
Will always be there.

To See

Running through life with blinded eyes,
The veils are many no matter the hue,
Ignorance, hate, bigotry and weight,
The blindfolds we wear are seen through by few.
Countless will look but never see,
The beauty inside of you and me,
Better than the biggest gem,
The sparkle is there behind the wall,
Hiding but never completely hidden,
A shine inherent to us all.
Countless will seek and hopefully find,
The path that truly unlocks their minds.
To see is to be fully alive,
And to become a part of humanity.
It is never too late,
We still can try,
To see our world as a community.
Search beyond every eye you meet,
For lying beneath is what I feel we seek.

*S*ome of the poems is this chapter were written while striving for happiness in limbo. Indeed, they were the sparks of hope that proved I would find some way to break free from my self-wrought prison cell, and I clung to them with all my strength. They were my lifeboats amid the raging storm that was myself.

When I began to wake up from my dark coma, I looked upon these poems with a new appreciation of their importance. Along with the determination and tough love of friends and family, whom I now take the time to thank with all my heart and soul for their support, my too few forays into positive poetry literally saved my life. I give my thanks to all those beside and around me on my journey towards hope and I give thanks to God, the Creator, the infinite intelligence or whatever or whomever stands above us for showing me that when it comes to bringing hope to the hopeless, the pen is indeed mightier than the sword. I leave you now, dear reader, with two two chapters of poetic healing and positivity.

Chapter 9

HEALING

Everyone Is Right

There once was a mind,
Who believed only he was right.
Arrogant and hateful he was,
As he walked alone in the night.
Though this mind was negative and hateful,
His heart secretly yearned for the light.
He let love in one day and found,
Everyone is right.
Whatever thoughts you think,
Know that everyone is right.
Our paths may all differ,
But know everyone is right.
Our changing thoughts and opinions,
Are simply steps toward the light,
Be they forward or backward,
I feel now everyone is right.

Individual

I made a mistake,
Many years ago.
I wrote, "We'll die the same."
Well, how can that be so?
We are each individuals,
We all have unique souls.
We live and die differently,
Many of our stories still untold.
I am now an individual,
Yet connected to all,
And I hope you are too.
So let us live and die as we please,
And to our own selves be true.

Found

The labyrinth I was in,
Was twisting and turning,
Confusing and distracting,
Full of negativity,
Wall to wall with sin.
As the haze began to clear,
And the walls to dissolve,
I found that inner resolve,
Courage, lightness and love,
Took the place of fear.
The end of the maze is near.

Spit

That old lightning bolt I ate,
Was made up of fear.
So I spit that thing out,
It is time to shift gears.
I needed room for some love,
I needed room for some light,
So I spit that bolt out,
And ended my inner fight.
I give thanks to that lightning bolt,
For keeping me going,
But I now spit that thing out,
For my love is now flowing.

Regeneration

I have now stopped,
Bleeding thoughts from my head,
There is regeneration taking place,
Each time I lay down to bed.
My old wounds are now healing,
Love is closing them up,
Worn bandages are coming off,
As moonlight and sunlight refills my cup.
A regeneration of spirit,
Is now occurring within,
New skin is being formed,
As I let go of past sins.

Letting Go

A new path has become clear,
I draw closer to it by the moment,
The way opened up when I chose to let go,
Of all of my pain, guilt, shame, anger and fear.
Letting go is easier by the day,
Letting go has shown me a new way,
Letting go has opened the doors of my heart,
Letting go is how I found a new start.
Detachment was tough for a man of proof and logic,
But I can tell you now,
That the new me feels fantastic.

Feathered Pen

A pen light as a feather,
Is easier to hold,
Its strokes are much smoother,
The creations more bold.
A feather given by a bird,
Or perhaps by an angel,
Is superior to one of iron,
It allows for new angles.
My new feathered pen,
Has released an old fear,
I now write with courage and love,
Without the need to shed tears.

Golden Soul

My old iron soul,
Was carrying too heavy a load,
So I had to renew it,
And make better use of it.
Like the alchemists of old,
I have now changed it to gold,
In a regeneration of spirit,
I released the darkness carried in it.
Like the blacksmiths of old,
I have now reforged my soul,
Putting an end to my dark night,
And moving upwards to the light

Air

Breath in the breeze,
Blown out by the trees,
Inhale and exhale,
That green given air.
Let it fill up your soul,
It will help you to care.
Gusting and swirling,
The healing winds come,
Embrace them joy,
And let your pain be undone.

Water

The rush of a river,
The ebb and flow of the seas,
Water can bring tranquility,
Help put a troubled mind at ease.
The roar of a waterfall,
The pulsing of waves,
If fresh they can bring life,
A soul they can save.
Empty and clean out your cup,
Then take a deep breath,
Before filling it back up.

Fire

Calm and controlled,
Or wild and wandering,
Its beauty can be gentle,
And strangely hypnotizing.
Fire can heal with its flame,
Or consume with its anger,
If handled with love,
It is certainly without danger.
It can give light to the darkness,
Bring warmth to the cold,
Be a meeting place for friends,
Where stories are told.

Earth

The sands of the desert,
The soils of the field,
If worked they give plenty,
Food does the earth yield.
The darkness of caves,
The peaks of the mountains,
Can help us to heal,
They are spiritual fountains.
Take care of the earth,
And it will protect you from harm,
Always giving of itself,
In the wilds and on farms.

Spirit

The energy that connects us,
It is light and it is love,
We all have it in us,
The glow from above.
It is unseen yet visible,
In laughter and smiles,
In heartaches and sadness,
Helping us through our trials.
Let us awaken our spirits,
Share what we find,
Embrace those who need it,
Leave none behind.

Soul

The center of our being,
What makes us unique,
The soul inside of us,
Our mountaintops peak
Only God stands above it,
Or Goddess if you like,
Whatever path you follow,
Let it fill you with light.
Being true to ourselves,
Being humble and kind,
Is what opens our souls,
And beckons us to shine.

Open Window

Draw the shades,
Open your windows.
Let in the sun,
Let in the rain,
Smell the breeze,
Let it take away your pain.
Reflect on the light,
As it dances with color,
Embrace the vibrations,
They are for you and all others.
Observe the true beauty,
Interpret the sensations,
Let your spirit be free,
To enjoy the Creation.

Ever Onward

I move ever onward,
In the moment of now,
With eyes that have been healed,
Without knowing how.
I sail ever onward,
With focus and intent,
Through moonlight and sunlight,
Hope was I sent.
I walk ever onward,
Connecting inner and outer,
Meditating when needed,
Done being a doubter.
I fly ever onward,
Towards peace and love,
A man of day and night,
Sending my gratitude above.

Gratitude

In two simple words,
There is a hidden power,
Can you guess the phrase?
Here is a moment to ponder.
Thank you,
For your patience,
Thank you,
For your time,
"Thank you" are the words,
That are linked to the divine.
They are words of respect,
They are words of healing,
There is perhaps only one other phrase,
That is imbued with more feeling.
Do you know those three words?
I am sure that you do,
Put together with "Thank you"
They form a beautiful combo,
Without further ado,
"Thank you. I love you."

Chapter 10

HOPE AND A FUTURE

A Change

There was a darkness before my dawn.
Looking back,
It see it was oh so very long.
I ran myself ragged,
Tied myself in knots,
Refused to move forward,
Glued to one spot.
Afraid of the sun,
Hiding from the light,
Hating my reflection,
Awake only at night.
Then suddenly one day I stopped.
Looked around,
And realized I was nowhere bound.
I transmuted my darkness,
Awoke to the day,
Basked in blue skies,
Felt some sun rays.
Walked along the water,
Laid down in the sand,
Inhaled some forest air,
Got back in touch with the land.
To those souls in despair I say,
Look forward,
The future is coming your way.
It is one of freedom and love,
Bright and beautiful.
And it is ours to create,
By free will and by fate.

Look for the Light

In the past I was blinded,
As I looked only for darkness.
I was cold and alone,
I was filled with selfishness.
As I opened my eyes for a peek,
I saw flashes of colors and light.
People now looked hopeful,
And I prayed for an end to my night.
That old smell of fear,
Was my own negativity,
Being reflected back at me.
I now look to the future,
And try to stay in the moment,
I now look for the moonlight and sunlight,
That we all carry in us,
And the future looks bright.

Never Alone

Your are never alone,
Even in darkness,
And in the light.
There are forces around you,
Making sure you are alright.
I am never alone,
Even in the day,
And in the night,
Protected by some force,
Seeing that I am alright.
We are never alone,
We are always connected,
At the level of spirit,
Our souls are in communication,
Even though we,
May be unable to sense it.

Home

I awoke **in a place**,
That I thought was long gone.
There was love in the air,
Pain had changed into song.
There were people all around,
Smiling and joyful they seemed.
They laughed in the sun,
And danced on moonbeams.
I looked on in wonder,
Thought I still slept,
A woman said, "Welcome Home."
And I fell down and wept.

A Lover's Touch

A lover's touch
Can stop any pain,
Put out any fire,
Shelter you from rain.
The caress of love,
Can bring hope from despair,
Shed light on the darkness,
Inspire you to care.
A lover's touch,
Can help bear any cross,
Raise up the damned,
Find those who are lost.

The Women

To the women of the world,
I say you have the power,
To cause the bloodshed to stop,
To make the warmongers cower.
Will you make a stand and say,
That enough is enough,
Tell the men to stop fighting,
It is your turn to be tough.
Say that peace is courageous,
There is little glory in death,
If enough of you do this,
You will take away the worlds breath.

The Men

Why do you keep fighting,
In the wars of the rich,
Is it to defend your homeland,
Or because you are unable to find a niche?
Search your soul you many find,
That the killing of another,
Is exactly the same,
As killing your brother.
The world is weary and needs rest,
To heal the wounds of those lost,
Let us put our weapons away,
And stop all this loss.

The Children

When problems abound,
And all hope seems gone.
When despair closes in,
And fear is all around.
When the pain seems too much,
And the lies grow too heavy.
When the people look skyward,
And need Gods touch.
Take heart everyone,
For then will come,
The guardians of freedom,
The Children of the Sun.
That time is now,
They are all here,
And they all know how,
To create Heaven on Earth.

Freedom

Freedom is inherent,
Our God-given right,
Without need to question,
Without need to fight.
This earth is for all
Each of us is free,
From the moment of birth,
To choose who we wish to be.
Let us take off our shackles,
Break out of our chains,
Change tyranny to peace
And begin healing our pain.

Stop War, Stop Death

The war machine is broken,
It is falling apart,
The soldiers want to go home,
For war they have lost heart.
The energy of Man,
The dream of a woman,
The intervention of **divinity,**
Stops War.
All the guns are thrown down,
The weapons torn apart,
The women tell their men to stop,
For war they have lost heart.
The energy of love,
The awakening of spirit,
The benevolence of strangers,
Stops War.
The cancers fade away,
The viruses break apart,
The sicknesses leave our bodies,
The diseases of Man have lost heart.
The energy of indigo
The ray of a recluse,
The spirit of newcomers,
Stops Death.
Our prejudices disappear,
Our hatreds fall apart,
Peace and love win the day,
For anger we have lost heart,
The power of peace,
The smile of a woman,
The strength of the stars,
Stops Death.

The Return of the Goddess

For far too many centuries,
There has been an imbalance.
A patriarchy ruled and reigned,
But soon now comes a great change.
The Return of the Goddess.
The reintegration of the feminine,
Into the structures of power.
Bringing balance back to the Earth,
And giving respect where it is deserved.
The Return of the Goddess.
But she never really left us,
Just was pushed to the background,
By dark forces seeking control,
Her return has been foretold.
The Return of the Goddess.
The return to full consciousness,
The earning of our birthright.
A new age is nigh,
Take a look to the sky.

The Age of Magic

The dream has come,
The time is at hand,
Spiritual awakenings,
Happening throughout the land.
The river of spirit,
Flows through us all,
Heralding the dawn,
The dark forces fall.
Fantasy becomes reality,
Wizards walk the land,
Healing with their magic,
Any who reach out their hand.
New inventions given,
By those from the sky,
Bring smiles and cheers,
And with joy some of us cry.
The Age of Magic is here,
Technology and Spirit,
Both creating miracles,
So go out and live it.

Uprooted

I once was a tree,
And thought I was free,
Never realizing,
I was rooted to the ground.
Standing strong in the storm,
Without seeking to conform,
Never realizing,
I was standing all alone.
So I uprooted myself,
Broke out of my cell,
Now realizing,
I am free to roam around.
Becoming human once more,
With muscles a little sore,
Now realizing,
I was born to explore.

An End To Why

Tired of questions,
Weary of riddles,
Done with, "why?"
Done with "Who am I?"
The answers I found,
Were buried deep within,
The truth was inside,
Anew I begin again.
Liking the new me,
More and more each day,
An end to why,
An end to "Who am I?"

Who I am

I am a poet,
A sinner and saint,
A dreamer and lover,
A son and a brother.
I am a creator,
Of words that form images,
Of phrases imbued with feeling,
Part becoming and part being.
I am now useful,
With words do I work,
I am getting better,
I am Lee Timmer!